/ piano

THE AUDITION SUITE

Four Comic Songs for Theatre Singers

ISBN 978-0-634-04655-1

HAL•LEONARD® CORPORATION
7777 W. BLUEMOUND RD. P.O. BOX 13819 MILWAUKEE, WI 53213

Visit Hal Leonard Online at
www.halleonard.com

Audition 101

Lyric by Martin Charnin

Music by Michael Dansicker

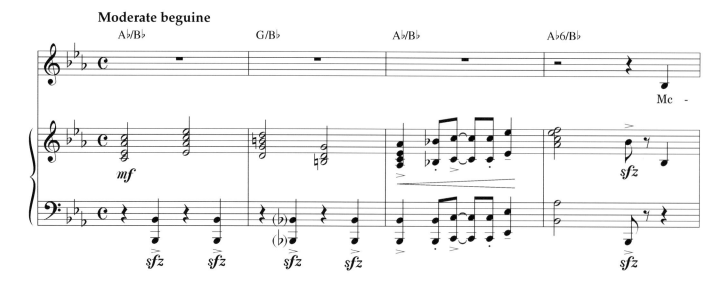

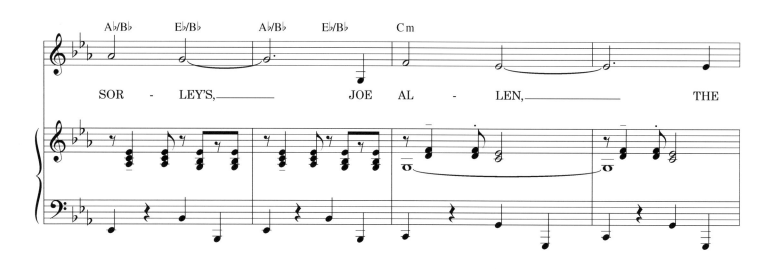

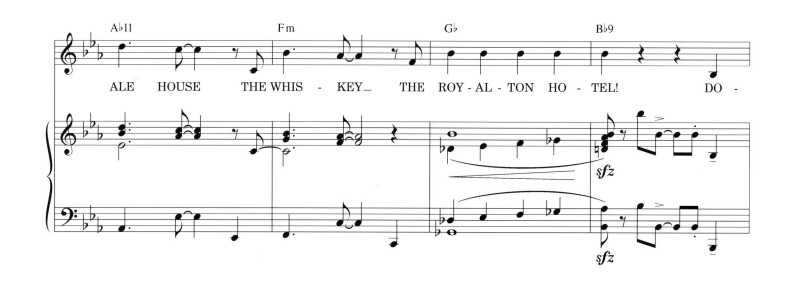

Confession

Lyric by Martin Charnin

Music by Michael Dansicker

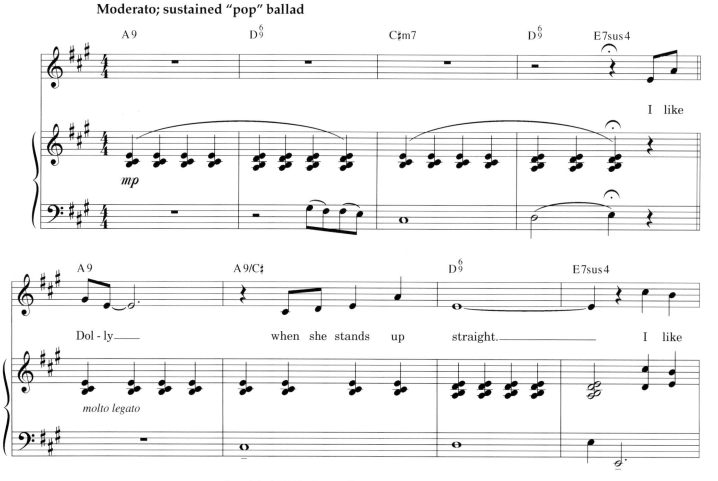

5

Family Tree

Lyric by Martin Charnin

Music by Michael Dansicker

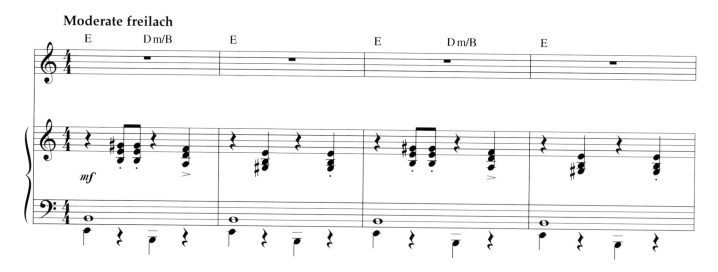

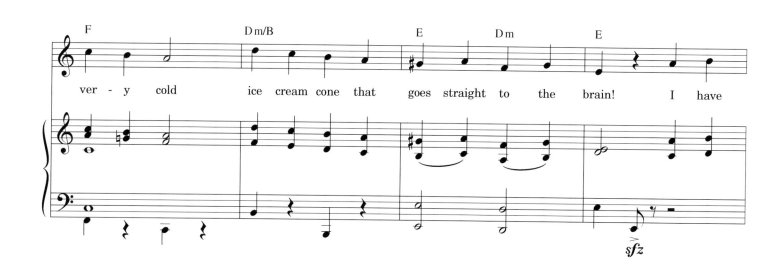

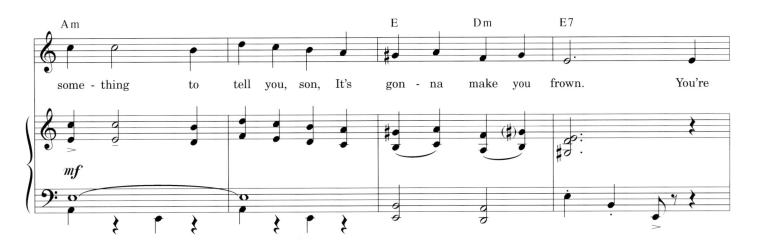

some-thing   to   tell you, son,   It's   gon - na   make you   frown.   You're

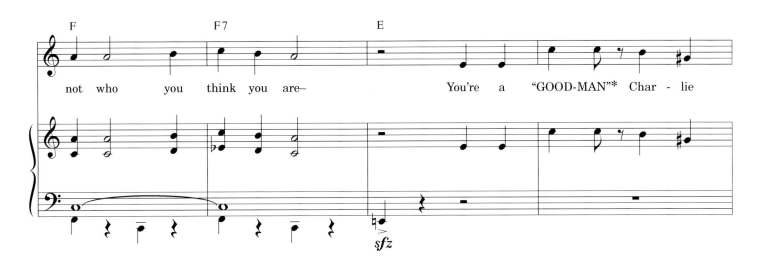

not who   you   think you   are—   You're a   "GOOD-MAN"*   Char - lie

Stringendo

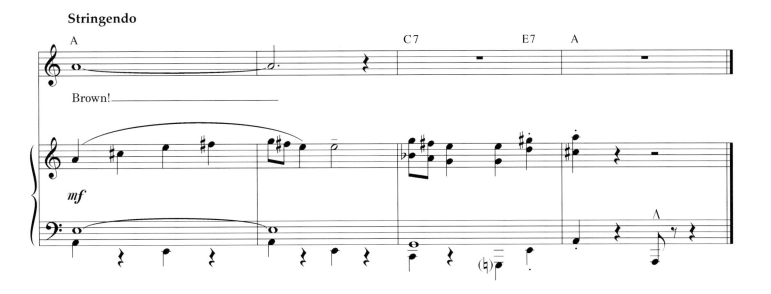

Brown!

* Note: pronounced GOODMAN - as in the family name.

Special Skills

Lyric by Martin Charnin

Music by Michael Dansicker